NEXT LEVEL
LEADERSHIP

FROM DISHWASHER TO FRANCHISE OWNER

21 LESSONS THAT TOOK MY CAREER TO THE NEXT LEVEL

TYRELL REED

YOU'RE READY! I CAN SEE IT IN YOU.

The real trick is seeing it in yourself and having the will to go get it. I built this course as a step by step guide to Next Level Leadership. With a new lesson, daily routine check, and action step delivered each day.

Get your mind prepared for 21 days of coaching & accountability. Each day will have a theme and content to dig a little deeper into each theme.

Here's what the 3 weeks will look like:

Phase 1 - Baby Steps & Mindset

Phase 2 - Routine is Everything but Organization is the Key

Phase 3 - All Business is People Business

When it's all said and done you will have designed your success and put together actionable steps to achieve your goals. Your team will appreciate your growth and reward you with their engagement. Your guests will notice the change and tell someone they've got to check out what you're doing. Give me 21 days and I will give you the foundation to create a fulfilling environment for you and your team.

Tomorrow starts your journey!

CONTENTS

DAY

1

"

DEFINITENESS OF PURPOSE IS
THE STARTING POINT OF ALL
ACHIEVEMENT.

Growth in any capacity begins with a mindset. A mental preparedness for the task to come. Understanding your abilities, your limitations, your motivators, and weaknesses are all of equal importance.

This week we will break down the mental aspect of leadership, design your future leadership style and life, get to know your personal strengths and talents, and develop a personalized plan for your leadership transformation.

FINDING YOUR REASON WHY IS THE FIRST STEP TO FINDING SUCCESS

What's your WHY? What is your reason for choosing to become a better leader?

Don't blurt out the first cliche' google searched "top interview question response". Really give this one some thought. What's your WHY? What is it that truly gives your life purpose and meaning? I can't answer that for you but I can tell you that for me the wellbeing of my family means everything to me. They are my reason for all that I do, and they are dependent on me. I will not let them down. Your WHY may be the same, or it may be different. What's important is that you know and understand your purpose.

If you're thinking "How would I even begin to know my purpose?". Well the answer is in you. You just have to ask yourself the right questions. Let's start here:

What excites you?

What are your strengths?

Where do you add the greatest value?

How will you measure your life?

When you can answer those, you can determine your purpose. Your purpose will be the center of your success.

Below you will find links to 3 assessments. These will help uncover your strengths and gain understanding of your personality traits and leadership style. Each takes just a few minutes and I encourage you to complete them as soon as possible so that we can dive into the results.

https://www.16personalities.com/

DISCOVER THE BEST PART OF YOURSELF

HIGH5 is a free strengths test that has helped +750 000 people to discover what they are naturally good at.

Get Yours (#)

https://www.123test.com/disc-personality-test/

DISC Personality Assessment

This free DISC personality test lets you determine your DISC type and personality profile quickly. Find out how the DISC factors, Dominance, Influence, Steadiness and Compliance predict your behavior towards others and the everyday things you do

Start Here (https://www.123test.com/disc-personality-test/)

DAY

2

"

WHAT YOU GET BY ACHIEVING YOUR
GOALS IS NOT AS IMPORTANT AS
WHAT YOU BECOME BY ACHIEVING
YOUR GOALS.

No, really. What does the mountain top look like for you? Knowing who we are is the first step now we must choose where those insights lead us. All great leaders understand the importance of goal setting. Achieving one's goals builds confidence and self worth as well as inspiring higher achievement in others. We'll pace ourselves with a series of "small wins" to build up our "can do" muscles. Knowing the harder work is ahead of us, it's important to train our minds to be positive and uplifting when times are tough. Wins do that!

Today's action is to watch the video below then work on your own set of goals using the worksheet below. Let's start with a set of short-term goals to get warmed up. First think about a 30-day goal. What can you accomplish in the next four weeks? Secondly a 60-day goal...besides finishing this course that is. Lastly let's work on something a little further out...with a 90-day goal. They can be personal or professional, that's all up to you. Try to have them sent to me before tomorrow's lesson.

https://www.youtube.com/watch?v=wGbmAH4mBPA

I love this overview of SMART Goals

Start your S.M.A.R.T. Goal planning with this worksheet. Click the link below

Download at www.tyrellreed.com/tools

DAY

3

"

SHOOT FOR THE MOON EVEN IF YOU
MISS YOU'LL LAND AMONG THE STARS
- E.P. ROSE

Great job creating those short-term goals! Knocking those down is going to be such a confidence builder for you. I want you to take that a step further though.

What do you really want from and for your life? Maybe it's a dream house or Lamborghini. Maybe you dream of extravagant vacations, or a restaurant tour around the world. Take some time to write out all the amenities of your perfect life. Now write them again 4 more times.

With these 5 sets of dreams, I need you to place them in 5 areas that you see every single day. (Mine are in my bathroom, my office, on my laptop, both cars, and in my wallet)

Today's action is to take your dreams and share them with someone you trust to hold you accountable to your goals. Someone that cares enough about you to tell you the truth (even when it hurts). Secondly, I want you to recite those dreams to yourself twice a day every day. Affirming your commitment to your future self.

https://www.youtube.com/watch?v=n-y_fgoAToc

Check out this video from Prince Ea

DAY

4

"

A **GREAT ATTITUDE** BECOMES
A **GREAT DAY** WHICH BECOMES
A **GREAT YEAR** WHICH BECOMES
A **GREAT LIFE**

When it comes to personal and/or professional development there are only three things that matter.

Knowledge - Do you have the know-how to get you to the next level?

Skill - Do you have the right skills to get you to the next level?

Will - Do you have the will to work for it? And the right attitude to push through the difficult moments?

The first two can be taught or improved. Your Will comes from within you. Your Will comes from your Why?

My favorite motivational speaker, Dr. Eric Thomas always teaches that average skill and a phenomenal will, will take you much farther than big talk, accolades, and all the shiny distractions that keep us from outworking our own expectations.

Listen carefully to the Guru Story from Dr. Thomas. It captures the essence of what it takes to be successful.

https://youtu.be/lsSC2vx7zFQ

Watch this and then decide for yourself how badly you want to breathe.

Today's Action

Recite your short-term goals out loud to yourself in the mirror. Look yourself in the eyes! It's important to affirm to yourself your ability to live out your dreams. Trust me...if you don't believe wholeheartedly in yourself no one else will either.

DAY

5

"

ALMOST EVERY SUCCESSFUL PERSON BEGINS WITH TWO BELIEFS: THE FUTURE CAN BE BETTER THAN THE PRESENT, AND I HAVE THE POWER TO MAKE IT SO.

Mindset is Everything

One of my favorite quotes is from Dr. Ben Carson's book, Think Big. Dr. Carson says, "Struggle is the process by which human beings grow wiser, more disciplined, fulfilled, and mature". I was 16 years old when that line first gripped me. So much so that I typed, printed, and framed a copy of those very words to hang on my wall. 20 years later it still hangs on the wall of my home office. I believe now even more than I did then that true growth comes from resistance. Adversity is life's greatest teacher...when you're in the right frame of mind to catch the lesson.

Google "mindset" and you're sure to come up with a billion references on why it's so key to success and true happiness. Dr. Carol Dweck is probably the leading educator on the subject. She has determined that mindset lives on an ever-evolving spectrum between two points. Fixed and Growth. The image below highlights some of the key characteristics of both.

Your action item for today is to determine your mindset and identify your key areas for growth. Below the image is a link to a short test to help you.

And if you're interested Dr. Dweck's award winning audio book, Mindset is available for free on youtube. Give it a search.

What's your Mindset (http://blog.mindsetworks.com/what-s-my-mindset)

https://youtu.be/kDHtyYlwM1A

DAY

6

"

SMALL WINS DAILY

THE SECRET TO MORE CONFIDENCE,
MOMENTUM & FULFILLMENT

Baby Steps = Small Wins

I'm sure you've heard the old saying "How do you eat an elephant?..one bite at a time." Well, how do you accomplish your goals? The same exact way! One task at a time. Baby Steps. You keep moving forward even if it's just an inch. Set yourself some milestones on the way so that you can reward the "Small Win". Then you keep it moving. When you are laser focused on the goal and you're progressing one task at a time eventually you'll look up and find yourself further along than you thought and closer to the win than you've ever been.

Today's action is to take your short term and long-term goals and break them down into baby steps. A critical part of success is understanding the process. Start with an end goal and reverse engineer your process all the way back to this very moment. Then ask yourself "What do I need to be doing today to reach my goal next month, next year, next level?"

Remember when you are crystal clear about what you want it's much easier to trace the steps needed to achieve. Vague goals are much harder to engineer because the process will lack clarity. So, know what you want and know what it takes to get it.

Like ET says in the video below. "Fall in love with small and blow up big!"

https://youtu.be/bnQYMMrKMRo

Win the Day! Each and every day!

DAY

7

"

LIMITS BEGIN WHERE VISION ENDS

Now that we've spent this entire week working on our goals, our strengths, our personality traits, and our mindset. It's time we bring all of those things within your grasp.

We're going to work on creating a vision board...but first let's answer a few questions:

1. What are your short-term goals?

2. What are your long-term dreams?

3. What are the baby steps required to reach those goals?

4. How will you use your strengths?

5. How will you celebrate each small win?

Below you'll find a link to my digital vision board. I created it using a free app called Canva (http://www.canva.com) and images from google.

I'll also include a youtube video to help generate ideas

Reed Vision www.tyrellreed.com/tools

https://youtu.be/kTYE3ZvXfXU

DAY

8

"

YOU'LL NEVER CHANGE YOUR LIFE
UNTIL YOU CHANGE SOMETHING
YOU DO DAILY. THE SECRET OF YOUR
SUCCESS IS FOUND IN YOUR DAILY
ROUTINE
- JOHN C. MAXWELL

Week 2 Day 1

Your Routine Will Define Your Life

It's been said that above all other things it is a person's daily routine that truly defines them. When I think about that, I truly believe it. It's those things that we do every single day that make us who we are. If you eat junk every day, then your body will show it no differently than if you were to work out every day. Warren Buffett made his fortune by reading for six hours every single day. His routine defined him as the most successful investor of all time.

Routines provide structure, builds good habits, increases efficiency, increases comprehension, saves time, and most importantly circumvents the need for that pesky thing we all lack. Motivation.

What's your daily routine look like? Is it an accurate depiction of who you are?

This week we will work on building our morning and evening routines for success. Focusing on positive habits and eliminating the time killers in our day.

Today's action is to write down 5 things that you do every single day.

https://youtu.be/SELWtQpcy1A

DAY

9

"

SOME PEOPLE DREAM OF SUCCESS
WHILE OTHER PEOPLE GET UP EVERY
MORNING AND MAKE IT HAPPEN

Do you know how successful people get more out of each day than the rest of us? They get up early! Really early! Most start their days around 4 a.m. and they all share a common theme. They get into their routines from there. I'm not going to tell you exactly what you need to be doing each day because we're all different and what works for me may not work for you. I can tell you that no matter what it is absolutely critical to begin your day with a win.

My mornings typically look like this:

5:30-6:00am - Wake up & drink a big glass of water

6-6:30 - Get kids ready for school

6:50 - Drop off

7:00 - Check bank accounts

7:15 - Update quickbooks

7:30 - Catch up on overnight email

8:00 - Weigh in & shower

9:00 - Leave for work

Now I'd really like to include 20-30 mins of exercise in my mornings to really supercharge my days.

What do the first two hours of your day look like?

Where can we optimize?

Are you planning your work?

Are you prioritizing the important tasks?

Are you planning for your team?

With just a few minutes every single day you can help everyone around you by having a plan and executing at a high level.

https://youtu.be/BLSR9WM9xx0

Wake Up

DAY

10

"

SUCCESSFUL PEOPLE DO DAILY WHAT
OTHERS DO OCCASIONALLY.

Yesterday we talked about the importance of starting your day off with wins. There's an even greater impact, an almost supercharging effect on those mornings when your evening routine sets you up for success. Let's face it...in today's hectic world there's very little about our days that we are completely in control of. Almost every single thing we do is dependent on someone or something else. Having routine gives us a sense of peace and control. Control over our mental space, control over our time, control over our energy. Now of course everyone's needs are different, therefore our routines will serve different purposes. I like to work on creative things in the evenings when my house settles down and I know I won't be distracted with phone calls and email. Some people may prefer to read, or have a hot tea. No matter what your thing is...it's more important that you have a thing.

Here's mine:

6:00pm - Family dinner (when we're all home)

6:45pm - Bath time for the kids

7:15pm - Homework and reading time

8:00pm - Bedtime for kiddos

8:30pm - 20-30 min workout

9:00pm - Shower

9:15pm - Meditation

9:30-10:30 - Reading and writing time

11;30-12:00 Lay it on down

Check out today's video on the evening routines of some of the most successful people in the world. I'm also going to include an episode from one of my favorite podcasts, The

Model Health Show, where Shawn Stevenson goes in depth on the science of routine. Only if you're serious of course.

https://www.youtube.com/watch?v=oCvaeTq5V_k

https://www.youtube.com/watch?v=CwcyluqJro8&t=2s

The Model Health Show

DAY

11

> "
>
> YOU DON'T RISE TO THE LEVEL OF YOUR GOALS, YOU FALL TO THE LEVEL OF YOUR SYSTEMS.
> - JAMES CLEAR

Make every workday a great day!

In the book, Atomic Habits, author James Clear writes "You do not rise to the level of your goals. You fall to the level of your systems."

Simply put, our habits are by far the highest value determinant in our success and in our failure. Good habits yield favorable results while failure is unquestionably the byproduct of poor habits. Often times in our daily lives we live in the grey area between success and failure. Living in our comfort zones, doing only those things we "like" with a smile. No one's keeping score so it's easy to look past those losses.

However, in our jobs we are constantly being measured, and compensated accordingly. The measurement is typically based around how well we execute the "system". Luckily, we already understand that execution at the highest level is based on our routines, and our habits. Remember what you do every day is what makes you who you are. Are you executing at a high level? Do you have a "system" for the system? Are you looking for ways to improve those systems?

https://youtu.be/k3Ls28qBT5c

Here's a good video on routines

DAY

12

"

DISCIPLINE...
IS CHOOSING BETWEEN WHAT YOU
WANT NOW AND WHAT YOU WANT
MOST.

Use the right tools.

Let's face it. Changing your mindset, your habits, your routines, and ultimately your life is no easy task. Change doesn't happen overnight. It's going to take us some time to get the results we're aiming for. Which means we're going to need a little help holding ourselves accountable. I'm a big fan of using the right tech to help. I mean as far as I'm concerned, I'm carrying around the most reliable accountability partner ever in my pocket. My cell phone. Always there, takes all my notes and messages, keeps track of my appointments and even reminds me when my bills are due. No one in my life works as hard as that phone. No need to carry around a bulky planner and notepad. Just pull out my phone and notes are instantly synced to my laptop.

I've recently started using a few apps to help install some new habits in my life. I thought I'd share them with you as well as some others that I use daily to be more productive. See the list below.

Side note I am an Iphone and google user

Habit building:

Shine Day app

Today app

Calendar:

Google calendar

Outlook calendar

Task Lists:

Google Tasks

Reading:

Audible

Fitness:

My Fitness Pal

Map My Fitness

Nike Run Club

Finance & Credit:

Mint

Wallethub

Credit Karma

Other Favorites:

Apple Podcasts

Marco Polo

Glide

I've found use in each of these and maybe you will too. Check them out and find out for yourself.

https://youtu.be/i2yHL_1m7rg

Success is in your routine

DAY

13

"

YOU ALWAYS HAVE TIME FOR THE
THINGS YOU PUT FIRST.

In Brian Tracy's best-selling book, Eat That Frog!, the author outlines 21 time management principles to help the reader work through procrastination. Focusing on identifying and completing the most important tasks in your day. Using the analogy of eating frogs as those difficult tasks in our day, the author challenges us to eat the biggest ugliest frogs first, making the rest of your day a breeze. Another book, The One Thing, by Gary Keller, the author challenges the reader to ask yourself a simple yet powerful question. "What is the One Thing I can do such that by doing it, everything else will be easier or unnecessary?" I recommend you read or listen to both of these great books. Both identify the same issues in our lives. Too much going on in heads and in our worlds. So much so that our priorities become clouded, and work never gets done. Taking the time to plan our days helps to identify our biggest and ugliest frogs to eat.

My challenge to you is to line your frogs up in order of importance and eat those boys up. You'll free up more of your time, get more done, and build a rapport among your peers as a super producer.

Check out Brian's video on the ABCDE method for prioritizing.

Side note: both audiobooks are available for free on youtube.

https://youtu.be/FKOMTZ7PPLg

Check out the ABCDE Method

DAY

14

"

THE KEY IS NOT TO PRIORITIZE
WHAT'S ON YOUR SCHEDULE, BUT TO
SCHEDULE YOUR PRIORITIES.
- STEPHEN R. COVEY

When I say let's optimize your daily routines, what I really mean is let's figure out which tasks we need to prioritize and which ones we need to say goodbye to. For example, if part of your morning routine includes a task like washing last night's dishes. You may find it optimal to move that task to the evening because we first know that our brains are primed for difficult tasks early in the day, and washing dishes is wasting part of our productivity. I use that example because this is one that I struggle with personally. I tend to put off those pesky emails for a few dishes that aren't really bothering anyone.

Today's action is to review your routines and fine tune them. Not just today but as frequently as possible, since increased productivity is the goal.

DAY
15

> **"**
>
> FOR EVERY MINUTE SPENT IN ORGANIZING, AN HOUR IS EARNED.
> - BENJAMIN FRANKLIN

Organization is the Key

Now it's time to work. We've worked on our mindset, and our goals. I'm even reading them every morning as part of my routine. How do we turn all that positive energy into results? By getting ORGANIZED. Yes that's right. Getting ourselves organized is the key to it all.

Why? Because organizing your mind, your home space, your workspace, and schedules earns us the most critical component of productivity. Your time. Yes, we will earn time to do all those things that we can't seem to ever find the time to do.

I'm not saying you have to go all Marie Kondo with it but understand that owning our time means we own our success.

"Success is a result of long-term planning and daily action. Good organization helps you gain control of your time so you can plan and complete the tasks needed to achieve your goals."

DAY

16

"

BEING BUSY & BEING PRODUCTIVE
ARE TWO DIFFERENT THINGS

Have you ever seen a chicken run around with its head cut off? Neither have I...but the thought of this act being compared to people who are terrible multi taskers scares me. We've all seen them...they look busy but really not getting a damn thing done. And whatever does get done isn't done well.

The fact is when we focus on a single task, do it well and move on. We find ourselves infinitely more effective. It is estimated that the human brain processes more than 40,000 thoughts per day yet is only capable of focusing on one at a time. We are designed for singular focus, and getting things done is a great habit to build. Focus on what's most important every single day and the rest will take care of itself.

Today's action is to plan your entire work week in to-do's. What's most important? What can be delegated? What can be eliminated? How much time does each task take and when will you do it?

https://youtu.be/JVt9_U9adRE

DAY

17

"

CLUTTER
IS NOTHING MORE THAN
POSTPONED DECISIONS
- UNKNOWN

What is Decision Fatigue?

Ever wonder why some CEOs wear the same color suits or shirts every day, or why Warren Buffet goes to the same Mc-Donald's drive thru with exact change for his breakfast every single morning?

It's because they've figured out that their brains are only capable of making a finite number of decisions each day before fatigue sets in. So in order to reserve that brain energy for those highest priority decisions they've made routines out of the small stuff and therefore gone on to use their genius for good.

Decision fatigue according to Wikipedia refers to the deteriorating quality of decisions made by an individual after a long session of decision making.

So what happens when our brains get tired of making decisions...we get impulsive or we do nothing. Both of which renders us virtually ineffective.

My tip for you is to clean up the clutter in your life. Whether it's at home, in the car, on your desk, or even your computer desktop. Understand that your brain makes a decision about everything you see...even that pile of old magazines no one's ever going to read again. You must decide every time you see them what your intention is for them. Keeping your life tidy and organized eliminates the need to make all those tiny choices every day. We're going to start by organizing our paper.

Today's action is to make a plan for your paper. Where does the mail go? What about invoices, and receipts?

Check out this article from Huffington Post

(https://www.huffpost.com/entry/the-best-decluttering-advic
e-weve-heard_n_5a0c8906e4b0b17ffce1ffb8)

https://youtu.be/Q5etToRxvW0

DAY

18

"

EVERYTHING HAS A HOME.

Have you ever needed something important but couldn't find it? No, I mean you know you have this key or this document because you literally just had your hands on it the week before…but today it's nowhere to be found. It was this type of personal chaos that drove me to get better organized. Looking for the birth certificates for our kids to get registered for school became an office and closet destroying adventure. Two days later I found them in an obscure banker's box under some invoices and unopened mail from 6 months ago. Talk about frustrating. It was at that moment I knew that I needed to get our things in order. We simply cannot rip our house apart every time we need something important.

The very baseline idea to organization to me is simple. "Everything has a home" we use it and return it to its rightful place. So that when we need said item in the future there's no search needed. Sounds simple right? Let me tell you it's not. First there's the task of deciding what's important enough to have space in your life. Then there's determining the optimal home for each item or group of items. Then finally there's communicating the system to the rest of your family or team members and adhering to it.

As a restaurant manager it's critically important to apply this principle to your operation. Making tasks like inventory counting and food ordering painless. How many times have you ordered a case of "whatever" only to find you'd had it on another shelf or in the wrong location? Drives me crazy too…I know.

Take an assessment of your shelves, cabinets, and other storage spaces. Does every item have a home? Or do they have 3 homes and an ever-changing resting place? Make a plan to set inventory in its rightful home to make your life much easier down the road.

DAY

19

"

CLEANING AND ORGANIZING IS A
PRACTICE, NOT A PROJECT
- MEAGAN FRANCIS

Take care of your workspace.

We've already learned how important organization is to our overall productivity. When clutter accumulates, our attention diminishes, and performance begins to suffer. Clutter doesn't just happen in our personal spaces. It's killing our performance at work too. Here's a snippet from an article from Gary Keller, author of The One Thing.

Organize Your Workspace

Have Everything You Need Within Reach – Take a careful inventory of everything you use on a regular basis to get things done at the office. Keeping these items at your desk or on your computer will maximize productivity and make organization easier.

Get Rid of the Non-Essentials – Clutter is a distraction. We're not saying that your desk needs to be a fun-free zone but cutting out non-essentials will make a workspace more functional and productive. If you haven't used something in the past six months, get rid of it or store it away somewhere off your desk and out of eyesight.

Put Paperwork in Its Place – Piles of paperwork are one of the biggest organization pitfalls. Instead of letting paperwork stack up, create a filing system that is based on the one-touch method. Make different files for each project or client, and when a document comes across your desk either act on it, trash it or file it away. Once the project is complete go back through the file and get rid of anything that isn't essential.

Organize your Virtual Workspace – Your e-mail is its own workstation. Organize it the same way you would organize your paperwork – files and a one-touch system. Apply the filing system to your electronic files as well. Another strategy to consider is to develop a time block for checking your e-mail only two or three times a day so it doesn't become a time-sucking distraction.

https://youtu.be/88MjoZalHpM

DAY

20

"

EVERYONE IS AFFECTED BY
THREE KINDS OF INFLUENCES:
INPUT
(WHAT YOU FEED YOUR MIND),
ASSOCIATES
(THE PEOPLE WITH WHO YOU SPEND TIME),
AND **ENVIRONMENT**
(YOUR SURROUNDINGS).
- DARREN HARDY

Product of Your Environment

"We are all products of our environment; every person we meet, every new experience or adventure, every book we read, touches and changes us, making us the unique being we are."

Which is exactly why I say we must protect our environment from anything that takes us in the opposite direction of our goals.

I'm sure you get it by now... Positivity is the fuel that drives us to success. In the same way that negativity slows us down. We've all witnessed that person kill the entire mood of a room without even saying a word just as we've seen people who can brighten anyone's day.

On this road we're traveling there will be setbacks, roadblocks, detours, traffic jams, accidents, and just about anything else you can imagine in your way. You will need to pick yourself up more than once. Your mindset will be what determines how many times you can take the "L" and keep going.

I'm very grateful for my circle...my 4 closest friends are successful in their fields of expertise, great husbands and fathers. Together we keep each other motivated, hold one another accountable, support each other's businesses and projects. Look at the people around you and think about how their energy affects your vision.

Here are some of the ways I control my environment

- ☐ Read the Bible daily
- ☐ Spending time with my family
- ☐ Keep toxic people out of my circle
- ☐ Always try to learn a few things
- ☐ Listen to music
- ☐ Listen to audiobooks
- ☐ Drink green juice

- ☐ Drink lots of water
- ☐ Talk to my closest friends frequently
- ☐ Avoid the news
- ☐ Limit social media time

And probably about 100 other things that I try to do in order to keep my vibe positive.

Who and what are the factors surrounding you? Are they holding you back or pushing you forward?

https://youtu.be/zCYES8n8RQE

Listen to Les Brown speak on the influence of our environment

DAY

21

"

YOU ARE YOUR ONLY LIMIT.

You Made It! Congratulations on reaching day 21! Hopefully you've taken away some valuable nuggets to grow you personally as well as your business. If you're like me and you're looking for a way to maximize then you're probably asking, "What's next T?"

Hire a coach!

I'm serious. Hiring a coach will take you to the next level in more ways than you believe. Hiring a coach that has been where you're going and done what you're trying to do is an absolute game changer.

If you wanted to go to the Cayman Islands would you charter a plane, and get behind the controls yourself? With no training, no maps, and no co-pilot to guide you?

Of course, you wouldn't! So, why would you attempt to navigate the business world with the same level of recklessness and disregard?

Hire a coach. I'm not even saying you should hire me. Find someone who is an expert at what you do and then hire them.

That's the fast track to the Next Level.